MW01251853

The Boy Who Couldn't Cry

The Boy Who Couldn't Cry

by Rowan Isaac

Illustrated by Matthew Soffe

Gingerbread Press

Published by Gingerbread Press
160 Kennington Park Road
London
SE11 4DJ

www.theboywhocouldntcry.co.uk
info@theboywhocouldntcry.co.uk

A catalogue record of this book is available from
the British Library

ISBN 0 9554198 0 8

Printed in England by Caric Press Ltd,
Bournemouth, Dorset

For Ray

Contents

A Cloudy Day

A cloud became frustrated, being blown around,
So decided to become a person, and walk on the ground.
"Now the wind cannot tell me which way I should go."
As he laughed and danced 'round a grassy meadow.

A farmer emerged with a big gun in his hand.
"Hey you, the naked guy, get off my land!"
He fired a shot to highlight his request,
And the cloud ran away rather distressed.

He reached a small village that was charming and quaint,
With pretty thatched houses, with sparkly white gates.
"This is perfect for a fellow who needs to unwind,
I imagine the people are gentle and kind."

He strolled with a dance into a nearby shop,
Which sold buttons and bread and huge lollipops.
The young woman serving gasped and then fainted,
When she saw the bemused cloud, standing there naked.

An old lady reverencing in the morning's fresh bread,
Brought her umbrella down, on the top of his head.
"Take that you pervert," she coughed with rage,
"Go put some clothes on, you should be ashamed."

Off the cloud ran for the second time that day,
If he wasn't such a happy cloud, he'd be rather dismayed.
He came by some clothes just hanging on a line,
"I've found a clothes tree," he beamed with pride.

Just as he'd fastened the last button on his shirt,
He was hit with a rolling pin, which really rather hurt.
"Get out of my garden, you blighter, you thief.
If my husband were here, he'd tear you like a leaf."

The cloud didn't hang around to hear much more,
And ran like the wind, just like before.
"These people are crazy and confused," thought the cloud.
"You can't own something that grows from the ground."

As he sat frowning, bewildered and troubled,
From somewhere inside him, thunder rumbled.
A whiff of fresh pie blew right up his nose,
It'd been hungry work, running in clothes.

Like a fat man climbing a mountain of pasta,
Or a geisha pursuing her pastry covered master
He chased down the source of divine smelling food,
With shaking knees, and covered in drool.

Resembling a bear in the baker's door,
He snatched two big pies, and then one more.
"Hey you beggar, you soap dodging slob,
You gotta pay for them, son, do you got a job?"

"A job? "Thought the cloud, confused once more.
"I don't know, what do they look like? Are they large or small?"

"You gotta work for me if you want something to eat,
Here's a brush: Get sweeping! You can start on the street."

Doris, his boss, had a heart of callous rock,
And worked him like a slave, every minute on the clock.
He had no time for frolicking and lazing in the shade,
As he was always too tired at the end of the day.

After a particularly gruelling day scrubbing the floor,
His hands were all cut, and his back really sore.
He looked to the sky, his eyes weary and red,
And in a very sad voice, full of longing he said,

"I wish I was a cloud again, blowing up and down,
At least I'd only have the wind, pushing me around."

Everlye

I remember the first time I fell in love,
It wasn't with a girl, or any god up above.
But with a magnificently green and golden trimmed tree,
Who was known to me as Everlye.

Heavenly Everlye, I'd whisper like the wind,
That rustled her leaves, to make my heart sing.
Heavenly Everlye, take me again,
To the top of the world, above birds and other men.

I'd sit on her lap, and just be pleased,
To feel her bark, and hear her breathe.
When I grow up I want to be just like you,
Strong and tall, peaceful and calm,
Ready to help others with an outstretched arm.

As I grew older I tried very hard,
To be like Everlye, and have a big heart.
But to me it didn't come at all naturally,
It must be incredibly hard, being a tree.

Then girls came along with their fleeting glees,
But I never found one as good as my tree.
'Til I was a little bit older and giving up hope,
I was stunned by a girl, with hair like oak -
Which rustled in the wind, and made my heart float.

She grew with the flowers,
And sang with the birds.
I adored her spirit,
And lusted her curves.

Emily, she was christened at the age of three,
After some goddess or mythical queen.
Heavenly Emily, I whisper like a breeze,
I wouldn't trade you for a million trees.

Lachrymose Pilgrim

Leonard the Cyclops was born with two eyes,
Reviled as freakish curse and a crime.
Taunted as Biclops who sneaked up and down,
With the eye of a demon, 'til he was chased out of town.

Herman the human was born with one eye,
Which disgusted his mother, who wished he would die.
Rejected, excluded, alone and dismayed,
He finally escaped from his village of bane.

And so they wandered with hearts full of woe,
The Lachrymose pilgrims searched for their low.
And rattle their dreams to clean their face,
That traces their thoughts with lines of disgrace.

Thirty-nine days of vagrant wander,
Through scorching heat and lavish thunder.
Purgatory anguish strangles their dreams,
As tired confusion heightens their grief.

On the next day astray, Fate's dice fell,
Whose invisible tremors, forced like a spell,
The weary travelers by torn, punished feet,
On the worn stone path, there the two did meet.

So different were their worlds that sowed their pain,
So the same were their hearts that reached in vain,
For a hand or a word to comfort their sleep,
As they recognized the other as the thief of their peace.

Their eyes tricked their judgment, to see only the red,
Of boiling resentment that raged through their heads.
Colliding with cruel and immense volcanic force,
Erupting in blood that wept from their pores.

Death carries off the poor wasted lives,
And leaves us to ponder the cruelness of eyes.
So easily impaired, when red curtains are down,
Over the windows – or window – so the soul can't see out.

Lapis Lazuli

Today little Winfred lost his soul.
He said he had it when he was feeding the ducks,
But after that
     .....nothing.
A wilful young man,
He hatched a plan,
To retrace his steps, and find it.

The ducks said,
"A girl with red hair -
       who skips everywhere -
Took it to share ice cream."

So off Winfred ran,
To Napoleon's van,
And the ice-cream with the revolutionary flavour.

"Excuse me, mister Man…
            …a person…
                        …you seen her..?"
Winfred spluttered,
            …out of breath…
                        …from his run.
"A girl with red hair –
            who skips everywhere –
She's got my soul, and I mean to find her."

The man's moustache twitched,
As his brain tried to fix,
The description, to an ice-cream flavour.

"Ah," he recalled,
"Chocolate and juniper –
            very peculiar,
But fitting to the girl, I fear.
Sapphires for eyes,
Picked from the night,
And a voice of silver perfume.
The grace of the moon,
The depth of the sky,
She's the enchanting
            Lapis Lazuli."

"Did you see where she went?
Or know where she's heading?"
And the man pointed towards the large fountain.

Sat on the ledge, facing the sun,
Lapis Lazuli quietly sung:
"A soul is a thing of beauty,
Beauty's perceived by the mind.
The mind is explained,
As a function of the brain,
But this I know to be a lie."

Winfred sensed his soul next to her,
He couldn't see it, but knew it was there.
"Excuse me," he said, with a cautious edge,
"But I believe you have something that's mine."

When she looked 'round, he felt his soul ripple,
For now that Winfred could see,
He'd questioned before the use for girls,
But now-

      -in her-
He'd found the purpose of living.

His anger evaporated to clouds of love,
Whose rain drenched Lapis Lazuli.
"Please keep my soul,"
He cried with elation,
"It's empty if it's not with you.

Like a stone it will have me fall to my knees,
Every time I think of your face.
Immersed in you it will be complete –

      You know true love never dies.
When our bodies decay,
Our souls embraced,
Will ascend as a star,
And burn with the ardent symphonic joy of the worlds."

Lapis Lazuli smiled a smile –

      A fox would smile,
To beguile a particularly docile,
And obtuse prey.

"Your soul isn't yours to offer,
There's greater forces than I.
You will take that back,
And together choose your path,
But its heart shall remain with me."

"The light of mine night,
Hath the heart of mine soul."
As he cried joyous tears
That tasted of gold.
But when he opened his eyes,
The girl was gone.
And his soul fell apart,
Without its heart.

Left like a shell,
With emotions of a corpse,
"Is this still love?"
Winfred thought.

- Moral for Morale -

It's a lesson to us all, not to leave one's soul,
Lying 'round or ignored.
A dormant soul is perfect prey,
For evil hands-
          -with wicked plans,
Or demons that come dressed as lambs.

Messard Fry

Messard Fry could only speak in tongues,
God only knows what he's saying half the time.

Eye Yam Um Egg Low May Knee Yak

Jeff St. Steel had an insatiable urge,
To be the mightiest and best in the whole uni-verse.
More powerful and dangerous than any before,
Rich, oppressive, but feared above all.

To aid his quest of world domination,
Jeff sought the help of a powerful Shaman.

"I want to stand apart from all other men,
To have dangerous powers none can transcend.
As rare and mighty as the mountains of Nepal,
But I bid you must make me feared above all."

The Shaman smiled then revealed a herb
He'd picked from the bark of the Evening Birch.
"Take this and you'll be tomorrow, transformed,
Rare and dangerous, but feared above all."

The next morning Jeff didn't feel at all very well,
So he went to the Witch in the hope of a spell.
"You've got infungled – linnet's – shadows disease,
It's incredibly rare, you must be pleased.
As it's so dangerous and as powerful as the ground,
I'm afraid there's no cure that's yet to be found.
You'll certainly stand apart with those disfiguring warts -
But with that hunched back and red skin -

You'll be feared above all."

A Passage On India

There's a very big buffalo
Drinking the water in my pond,
I hope it rains soon,
Cos it's nearly all gone.

There's a monkey eating mangoes
From my prize winning tree,
I hope it dies soon,
So there's some left for me.

There's a man with no limbs
Pestering me for change.
We all beg for change – I tell him,
Just yours is from mange.

But, tell me if I gave you
All the change in my purse,
Would it be your greatest day of begging,
Or simply a curse.

Would you buy yourself a house,
A girl and a goat,
Or set off round the world,
In a shiny new boat?

Some would say you'd just go
Spend it all on grog,
Or waste it on betting
At the horses or dogs.

Maybe you'd buy food
For yourself and your cat,
Well you've put me off mine,
So you might as well eat that.

The Lamentations of Eli Maurai

In a small village,
In a remote little town,
Just off the coast of Ireland
And drifting further down,
Is the floating island of Fennakye
Where one Eli Maurai is trying to cry.

At thirteen years of age
And not a tear to his name,
He's starting to worry
He might be insane.

He jumped off a bridge
In the hope it would fix,
His red raw eyes
So longing to cry.

Incinerated his favourite toys,
Four wooden soldiers from his Uncle Roy.

Butchered Colossus the family dog,
With a rusty old knife he'd found in his sock.

Squeezed raw onions in his eyes,
Followed by pins and his blood stained knife.

"Any of these acts would make a sane boy cry,
A different tactic, I must try."

Whilst Eli slept,
A Puckish hand placed,
A wicked plan storming
Through his brain of grace.
The sordid plan ripened like poisonous fruit,
Filling his head with its toxic juice.

Eli woke from his sleep with a cheer,
And a smile that sneered from ear to ear.
"I have a stupendous, faultless, fabulous idea –
I'll steal other people's tears."

Out the front door to the most colourful day,
Eagerly Eli eyed for his prey.
It wasn't too long before he saw his first chance,
A pram with a baby, outside a bank.

The babe enriched with nature's virtue,
And serenity's smile; content and true.
He clutches his doll, whose mirrored glee,
Reflects their tacit harmony.

He tore the doll from the baby's embrace
And ripped the head off in front of his face.
The cruelest mind twisted with spite,
Couldn't stand to witness such brutish sights.

The baby paused before he screamed,
As he fought to process the horrific scene.
The look of shock was washed away,
As anguished tears ripped the floodgate.

Eli had prepared a leathery tin,
Which he held against the baby's chin,
To collect the weeping, gushing grief,
For the lamentable potion in Eli's dream.

When the mother rushed out to answer the call,
Of the weeping baby in torments shawl.
Wondering at the doll, lying on the ground,
"Whatever happened to this quiet little town?"

Now Eli's wicked grin
Resembled horns on a face of sin.
"I feel so alive when I make people cry,
It makes laughter sound coarse and undignified."

He saw his best and only friend Dee,
Sat on the branch of the old witches' tree.
Like a walking snake he crept up behind him
And pushed with a force that was nearly blinding.

He fell to the ground like pounding meat,
Gashing his side and twisting his feet.
He screamed and wept with such a din,
That he failed to notice Eli's tin,
Pressed lightly against his gushing eye,
Collecting the tears he'd mournfully cried.

"That's two victims now, maybe one more,
I need someone older, who's seen pain before."
Walking past a field of moss and rocks,
He saw a weathered old man, walking his dog.

Eli hid behind one of the stones,
And waited for the man with the shaking bones.
Now luck smiled on Eli just then,
As a stick for the dog landed on his head.

When the dog panted over to look for the stick,
Eli acted fast, and grabbed the dog quick.
Tying him up and clamping his jaws,
He put the stick in his own mouth, and got on all fours.

The old man's reaction was a confused, startled groan,
As Eli emerged with the stick he'd just thrown.
"Bleacher, my loyal, beloved old mate,
Have mischievous fairies queered your shape?"

When the old man bent down to inspect Eli,
His dignity cracked, and he began to cry.
As the weather beaten man carried his new dog away,
Eli smiled at a most successful day.

In his room, Eli lifted his potion with pride,
Then drank every last drop, till the glass was dry.
Just as he'd finished, he felt a sudden, searing pain,
That rushed through his body, that rattled his veins.

For a week the illness had him tied to his bed,
And everyday pleaded he could cry instead,
Of feeling this feeling that couldn't be described.
But it was on the seventh day, when one Eli Maurai died.

Who Is I?

I hope when
I die
I go to heaven.

When
My body's in the ground, and
My souls in heaven,
I wonder where
I'll be.

Kallou

I have lots of friends,
But there is one that will always be,
Not necessarily better, or gooder than the rest,
Just the goodest and best for me.

Kallou – Ibrahm – Cothlewait – Ga'dor.
I think he's foreign,
In fact I'm sure.
Sometimes in the playground
When you shout out his name,
Glue – broom – Cot – Wag – Door,
It sounds all mungley,
So it's Kallou for short.

I consider myself tolerant,
And fairly inclined,
But there's one boy I don't like,
With a dark cloud for a mind.

Malcolm or Leonard - I can't remember his name,
A stone thrower,
A name caller,
Just a general pain.

I don't talk to him,
And pretend not to hear,
When he calls me a wally,
Or maliciously jeers.

Not like when me and Kallou are together,
We know each other's thoughts,
And so talk hardly ever.

Kallou lets me know when my hair's in a mess,
Or my socks don't match my vest.
Leonard just tells me I look stupid all the time,
Doesn't he know I have feelings inside?

"One day," said Kallou,
"I must get on a plane,
And go to a place,
Where there's not much rain."

"Don't go," I cried,
Tormented inside.
"Hanging from trees
And hunting for bears,
Won't be as fun
If you're not there."

"Play with Leonard
And show him our tree,
And soon you'll see,
He's no different from me."

"He's not like you,"
I said to Kallou.
"His hair's not frizzy
And he always wears shoes.
He only wants to be bad,
And make people sad,
I can't be friends,
With such a cad."

"Give him a chance –
Be patient and kind,
All people are nice,
Somewhere inside."

Like all wise optimists,
With faith in other men,
They turn out to be wrong,
Again and again.

When I showed Leonard
Mine and Kallou's tree,
He tore off a branch,
And threw it at me.
I don't so much mind,
The graze on my face,
But our poor tree lost an arm,
What a disgrace.

I don't think he understood
Hunting for bears,
I'm not very grizzly,
Or covered in hairs.
We never used real traps,
Or actual guns,
And it wasn't as violent,
And a lot more fun.

The Doctor said, "You'll be walking soon,
And right as rain,
Just don't make any friends,
For a couple of days."

The Goat Paradox

I Like Goats,
Goats like oats,
Oats like rain,
But I Don't.

Doctor Morphia

Doctor Morphia composes in his lab,
Brilliant potions
and lotions
for scabs.

Whizzing bees, puffs of green,
Purple gushes of blue tasting fluffers.
Blossom clouds shattered and ruptured in tatters,
The song bird arose from his hand in scatters.

"Hooray is the day this bird of mine flay,
Whose wings are tinged a goldeny grey,
To I and all – the Fruit-Berry Jay.
May all who see her,
Gracefully sleep."

In the secretest cupboard in the secretest room-
next to the Grail and a dancing spoon,
He lifted the crown of Winter and May,
"Now is your song, Fruit-Berry Jay."

With trails of silk soared the bird of prayer,
The Doctor danced and pulled at his hair.
Ten long years locked in his cave,
Conquering nature and curing plagues.
"The Fruit-Berry Jay will cure with its song,
The world that heaves and weeps-

   whose vilest plague refuses to cease."

"The Fruit-Berry Jay, away, away,"
Whose wings filled the sky-

   with colours of her cry,
The song that fizzed from her tangerine beak-
in roses, yellows, and crystalline clouds.
Raced through air, forests and creeks,
"Rejoice the song that rings the day,
Away, away, Fruit-Berry Jay."

Through and forever the relentless night,
Fruit-Berry Jay sang and swayed-
                and sprayed her colourful song of light.
Then rose the sun that froze the Jay-
                whose curing song was sung and done.

Then every person that was being, simply ceased,
And all was happy-
and the world was at peace.

The Disappointed Fish-Hen

A lonely goldfish watched the hens
Chatter and natter and squabble and cluck.

"If I could be a hen for just one day,
I'd use my wings to fly away.
I wouldn't sit around here and chatter and cluck,
With the other silly hens, and the boring ducks."

He blessed the ground, the moon, the sky,
The sun, the water and the stars divine.
'Til one morning his prayers were answered,
As his mind arrived,
      In a hen's feathered hind.

The ecstatic Fish-Hen, short of time,
Gathered itself for its flight sublime.
"Here I come mountains, here I come clouds.
Here I come oceans, forests and towns."

He picked a flat spot for his runway to freedom...

...He flexed his wings and steadied his breathing...

...then...

...ran...

As you can imagine,

The rest of the day

Was rather disappointing.

The Hermit Crab

I found out on Thursday
That I'm not at all that tall,
But that everybody else is incredibly small.

Soon after I noticed
My hearing really isn't bad,
But that everyone speaks very quietly, in fact.

Before long it was clear
I'm not as clever as I thought,
It's just nobody thinks very hard anymore.

Then last night as I gazed at the stars,
I started to think in umms and ahhs,
'What if stars are close and not really that huge,
But tiny little windows -
some other light shines through.'

My mouth opened to the size of space -
as I thinked,
'I wonder if there's life somewhere up there,
Above the air,
On a planet some place in space.'

Then I frowned with remorse
As my mind changed course.
"I wander if there's life down here,
The evidence still is very unclear."

My thought was true, and is,
Even if my thinking became wrong.

I reflected morosely for what seemed like a year,
More closely, I guessed, was nearer.

When I looked back at the stars
They weren't the mystical bodies anymore,
Their charm and magic was eternally slurred.
And all I could see through the blackness and dust,
Was infinity only inferred.

Lamentations of Eli Maurai – Epitaph

His body was lowered in the dark, restful ground.
A pipe played coldly, and a small crowd stood around.
By drinking their sadness, the whole town was saved,
They would no longer suffer, or again be afraid.

As they looked at the box where Eli presided,
Not an eye was dry, or friendship divided.
Slowly their tears hit the wood with a thud,
Then faster and more grievous, till the soil was mud.

The tears they shed,
Made Eli's bed.
The thanks they gave,
Was his teary grave.

The Owl

The Wise Owl Lives Alone -
Unlike the Happy Badger.